In this corner... Dennis the Menace

"DENIS, LA PETITE PESTE"

"DENNIS DIE KARNALLIE"

"DANIEL EL TRAVIESO"

"STICKAN"

"MILLIPETER"

"VILLE VALLATON"

"DANIELE IL BIRICHINO"

"HENKIE HET HUISGEVAAR"

"KLEIN EDE"

"SOMBRINHA"

"DENNIS THE MENACE"

At an age when most children have trouble with English, Hank Ketcham's roving "Ambassador of Mischief" — Dennis the Menace — is amazingly fluent in a battery of languages besides English.

Indefatigable, irrepressible, and equally irresistible in Spanish, Dutch, Swedish, and Japanese, Dennis has set his own record in international understanding. His panel, distributed by the Hall Syndicate, appears in foreign newspapers in 37 countries abroad as well as hundreds of American newspapers coast-to-coast.

IN THIS CORNER... DENNIS THE MENACE is the latest report on this pint-sized playboy of the wide, wide world.

In this corner . . .

DENNIS
THE
MENACE

by Hank Ketcham

A FAWCETT CREST BOOK

FAWCETT PUBLICATIONS, INC., GREENWICH, CONN.
MEMBER OF AMERICAN BOOK PUBLISHERS COUNCIL, INC.

A Fawcett Crest Book published by arrangement with Holt, Rinehart & Winston, Inc. and the Hall Syndicate, Inc. This edition contains 62 additional cartoons that did not appear in the original Holt, Rinehart & Winston edition.

Ninth Fawcett Crest printing, October 1967

Published by Fawcett World Library,
67 West 44th Street, New York, New York 10036
Printed in the United States of America

"DAD! THAT DARN OL' MISTER WILSON SQUIRTED ME BACK!"

"WHO NEEDS A SALAD?"

"HOW CAN I HAVE A GOOD TIME IF YOU'RE GONNA COUNT MY HOT DOGS?"

"HEY, TOMMY! YOU AN' BILLY AN' JOEY AN' MARGARET AN' BETTY WANT A HOTDOG?"

"I'LL TELL YA WHY THE POOR KID'S EATIN' SO MANY HOTDOGS:
HIS FOLKS ARE *VEGETABLETARIANS!*"

"BOY! THAT'S *MY* KIND OF A HOUSE!"

"SEE? I *TOLD* YOU OUR GARBAGE DISPOSAL
COULD DO A ROOT BEER BOTTLE!"

"BOSS WANTS YOU!"

"GET YOUR HATS! I'M GONNA TREAT FOR ICE CREAM SODAS!"

"MOM'LL BE DOWN IN A MINUTE. SHE'S FILLIN' THE BATHTUB."

"WHO **SAYS** IT'S MY BEDTIME?"

"YOU, HUH?"

"I'M TRYIN' TO FIGGER OUT WHY IT GETS DARK."

"DID YOU KNOW THESE LITTLE ROUND THINGS SCREW RIGHT OUT?"

"*SURE* THEY'RE FIGHTIN'! HE'S A SOLDIER, ISN'T HE?"

"I SURE FEEL SORRY FOR GIRLS! DRESSES, HAIR RIBBONS, DOLLS... *BROTHER!*"

"WELL? YOU GUYS GONNA PLAY FOLLOW THE LEADER, OR AREN'T YA?"

"DID YA BUILD THE BATHROOM YET?"

"P'LICE DEPARTMENT? I WANNA REPORT A
CEMENT MAN WHO TRIES TO HIT LITTLE KIDS!"

"YOU EXPECT ME TO STAY IN BED WHILE A HELICHOPTER MISSES OUR HOUSE *THIS MUCH*?"

"WHO TOOK THAT CHICKEN LEG THAT WAS IN THE 'FRIGERATOR?"

"EASY, BERT! YOU CAN'T GULP THEM RELAXIN' PILLS LIKE CANDY MINTS!"

"MR. WILSON PAINTED HIS PORCH THIS AFTERNOON. HOW DO YOU LIKE THE COLOR?"

"WE HAVE LOVELY NEIGHBORS. THE LITTLE BOY NEXT DOOR IS A *DARLING!*"

"KNOW WHAT I BEEN DOIN' FOR YOU WHILE YOU BEEN SICK, MR. WILSON? I BEEN KEEPIN' YOUR CAR GREASED!"

"WELL, GEE! THE BIRDS AREN'T USIN' IT!"

"THAT'S A LOT OF FOOD FOR TWO PEOPLE."

"DAD! DON'T YA WANT YOUR PICTURE TOOK? DAD?
HEY, DAD!"

"GOSH! WHO'D EVER THINK THERE WAS A WHOLE BLOCK OF TOOTHPASTE IN A LITTLE TUBE LIKE THIS?"

"AW, HOW THE HECK DID YA KNOW IT WAS *ME?*"

"'I WOULDN'T SWIPE COOKIES IF YOU'D HAVE *LUNCH* ON TIME.' *THATS* WHAT I SHOULDA SAID!"

"WELL, IT SURE *LOOKED* LIKE A FLYIN' SAUCER!"

"I'VE BEEN SITTIN' UP HERE THINKIN'
ABOUT THE GOOD OLD DAYS!"

"I THINK YOU'RE WRONG, DAD! A HORSE IS *LOTS* BIGGER!"

"OKAY, YOUR DAD CAN CHIN WITH ONE HAND. *MY* DAD CAN CHIN WITH ONE *FINGER!*"

"...AN' HE COULDN'T HIT IT, AN' HE COULDN'T HIT IT! SO HE SAID A BAD WORD AN' HE *KICKED* IT!"

"YOU GOTTA ADMIT IT'S A PRETTY SAFE PLACE TO KEEP THE CAR KEYS!"

"YOU MEAN THEY MAKE. THIS SOUP OUTA *BIRD NESTS?*"

"THAT THUNDER IS MAKIN' MY EARS NERVOUS!"

"LET'S JUST WATCH FOR AWHILE. WE DON'T SEE HIM LIKE THIS VERY OFTEN."

"SO LONG, SLAVES!"

"YOU SHOULD GO AT NIGHT SOMETIME. EVERYBODY JUST *SITS* THERE!"

"I'LL TELL YA WHERE THE BILLS COME FROM:
THE MAILMAN BRINGS 'EM!"

"THEY WON'T LET ME HAVE ANY ROOT BEER. THAT'S WHY I'M SO WEAK."

"HER NAME? WELL, IT'S..UH...IT'S BESSIE. YEAH. BESSIE IS YOUR COW, DENNIS."

" CAN YOUR KID COME OUT AN' FIGHT?"

"GET YOUR RED HOTS!...I *DID* PUT MUSTARD ON IT...GET YOUR RED...BEAT IT, KID!...GET YOUR...*LISTEN*, KID!..."

"NO, HE *DOESN'T* HAVE TO GO TO THE BATHROOM. THE COACH
IS TAKING HIM OUT OF THE GAME!"

"ALL I'D HAVE TO SAY IS, "I WANT A ELEPHANT,"
AN' MY GRANDMA WOULD BUY ME ONE!"

"WHY GET SORE AT ME? YOU LOOK *GOOD* WITH GREEN EYEBROWS!"

"NEXT TIME I SNEAK YA SOME LIVER, *EAT IT!*
DON'T DRAG IT AROUN' THE ROOM!"

"YOU'RE *WRONG,* DAD! SHE LOOKED RIGHT
AT IT AN' IT'S STILL RUNNIN'!"

"I JUST WANTED TO SEE IF THEY *EVER* SLEEP!"

"IF HE'S THE KIND THAT SNEAKS IN THE CLOSET AND HAS BABIES, MY DADDY WON'T LET ME KEEP HIM."

"AW, MOM, THE SUN IS SHININ', THE AIR IS NICE...
WHY DON'T YA COME OUTSIDE AN' *LIVE* A LITTLE?"

"COOKIES! COOKIES! COOKIES! DON'T YOU EVER THINK ABOUT *ME*?"

"SURE, I'LL TELL YOU WHY HIS HAIR IS FULL OF NICKS.
HE'S FULL OF JUMPS."

"HE WAS BAD TODAY. HE GROWLED AT A SEEIN' EYE DOG!"

"THIS IS NOTHIN'. YOU SHOULDA SEEN IT SNOW WHEN I WAS *YOUR AGE!*"

"BOY! NOW, IF WE COULD ONLY *THROW* IT!"

"HI, MRS. WILSON! THIS SURE IS HOT CHOCOLATE WEATHER, ISN'T IT?"

"GEE WHIZ, MR. WILSON! I *SAID* 'DUCK'!"

"... AND WHEN THEY GET REAL COLD, THEY'LL GET UP AND FIX US SOME BREAKFAST!"

"BAD NEWS, HENRY. IT SEEMS RUFF MISSED HIS RAW EGG IN MILK THE LAST COUPLE OF DAYS, SO THIS MORNING...."

"THEY SURE KILLED HIM WHEN HE WAS *LITTLE*, DIDN'T THEY?"

"YOU SHOULDN'T OUGHTA SAY 'AIN'T', JOEY. IT'S BAD GRAMMAR."

"YEAH, I KNOW IT'S A BRAND NEW TABLE. DID YOU KNOW THAT'S A BRAND NEW HAMMER?"

"...'WASH YOUR HANDS! DRINK YOUR MILK! TAKE YOUR NAP!'
DON'T YOU SEE WHAT SHE'S DOIN'? SHE'S *BOSSIN'* US!"

"HEY, MISTER! WILL YOU TAKE A MESSAGE TO THE OUTSIDE WORLD?"

"IT COULD HAVE HAPPENED TO *ANYBODY!*"

"BE MY GUEST!"

"OF *COURSE* IT WAS AN ACCIDENT! YOU DON'T THINK I'D DELIBERATELY HIT THE BOY, DO YOU? DO YOU? *WELL, DO YOU?*"

"I WAS JUST SITTIN' THERE, KEEPIN' CLEAN, WHEN THIS KID SAYS, 'HI!, SISSY!'"

"REMEMBER YESTERDAY WHEN I ASKED YA NOT TO SPANK ME?"

"OH YEAH? WELL. YOU STAY IN!"

"OPEN THIS DOOR AT ONCE!"

"DIDN'T WORK."

"NOTICE THE BIG ROOM, AN' THE SWELL FURNITURE, AN' THE 'LECTRIC BLANKET? *NOW* I'LL SHOW YA *MY* CRUMMY ROOM!"

"I DON'T NEED TO RELAX, DOCTOR! *HE* NEEDS TO RELAX!"

"MOM! I JUST WHAMMED A BURGLAR
WITH MY . . . . . WHERE'S DAD?"

"I DON'T WANNA SEE 'EM! I'M NOT IN THE MOOD FOR COMPANY!"

"Pssst! If you find a yo-yo in there, it's *MINE!*"

"COME ON! IF RIN-TIN-TIN CAN DO IT, *YOU* CAN DO IT!"

"YOU'RE GONNA HAVE TO *MOVE*, MISTER! WE'RE BUILDIN' A _FREEWAY_ THROUGH HERE!"

"NAW, WE DIDN'T HAVE ANY FUN! WHO WANTS TO SIT ON
A PARK BENCH AN' LOOK AT GIRLS?"

"THERE! HOW's *THAT* FOR A FISHIN' POLE?"

"YACK, YACK, YACK, YACK!"

"DAD, WILL YOU HELP US MAKE A DIVIN' BOARD?"

"THAT'S A HORNET'S NEST, SON. JUST LEAVE IT ALONE AND THEY'LL LEAVE US ALONE."

"I DON'T SEE NO CHIP ON HER SHOULDER!"

"WOW! WHOSE SHOES ARE IN *THAT* BOX?"

"I KNOW *ONE* THING SHE CAN'T BLAME ON ME: THAT *LOUSY CAKE!*"

"MY DAD'S GOT A BIGGER *MOUTH* THAN *YOUR* DAD!"

"I WAS SHOWIN' RUFF YOUR BOWLIN' BALL AN' IT CAME DOWNSTAIRS!"

"OH, RUFF! HAVE I EVER TOLD YOU HOW SWEET *YOU* ARE?"

"SURE LIKE TO EAT WATERMELON OUTDOORS. YA DON'T
HAVETA SAVE THE SEEDS!"

"NEXT TIME WOULD YA ASK THE GUY
TO PLAY A FEW COWBOY SONGS?"

"WHATTA YA MEAN SHE'S REALLY GOT LEGS? DON'T *EVERYBODY* HAVE LEGS?"

"A *RANCH* HOME!? WHERE THEY GONNA KEEP ALL THEIR COWS AN' HORSES AN' STUFF?"

"IT'S A GOOD LITTLE SCOOTER. HE GETS ABOUT THIRTY-FIVE MILES TO A PAIR OF SHOES."

HE'S PART GREAT DANE, PART BLOODHOUND, PART IRISH SETUP... AND *ALL MINE!*"

"WANNA SEE WHAT MY BIRTHDAY LOOKS LIKE?"

'YES, SIR. IF THAT' OL' GIANT WAS *THAT* TALL, HE COULD LOOK RIGHT IN THAT WINDOW!'

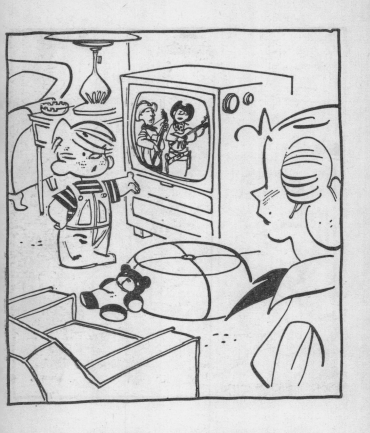

"HEY, MOM! *WHO'LL* BE COMIN' 'ROUND THE MOUNTAIN WHEN SHE COMES?"

"I KNOW YOU'RE NOT ASLEEP. THE TELEVISION IS STILL *WARM!*"

"I DON'T *WANT* A LICK!"

"IF YOU THINK *YOU'VE* HAD A TOUGH DAY, WAIT'LL YOU TALK TO *MOM!*"

'I HOPE YOU HEARD THAT PART ABOUT ' FORGIVE 'EM, 'CAUSE THEY DON'T KNOW WHAT THEY'RE DOIN' '?"

"I *KNOW* HE THINKS I'M SKINNY, BUT HE'S GOT TO STOP PUTTING PEANUT BUTTER SANDWICHES IN MY BRIEFCASE!"

"DON'T HE SHAKE HANDS GOOD, MR. WILSON? THAT'S MUD. HUH? DON'T HE SHAKE HANDS GOOD?"

"LITTLE KID GOT HIS FOOT CAUGHT IN THE
GLOVE COMPARTMENT OF HIS DAD'S CAR!"

" 'BOBBY SMILED AT HIS BABY SITTER. SHE WAS A
LIVING DOLL! TALL AND SHAPELY'... SAY, WHERE DID YOU
GET THIS COMIC BOOK, DENNIS?"

"I NEED ANOTHER BLANKET! *SOME* PEOPLE DON'T HAVE *'LECTRIC* BLANKETS, YA KNOW!"

"SHE'S *REALLY* SLEEPY THIS MORNING! LOOK... *COFFEE!*"

"RUFF WAS JUST TRYIN' TO HELP! HE WAS DUSTIN' THE TABLE WITH HIS TAIL!"

"IT SURE LOOKED LIKE AN EASY TRICK ON TELEBISION.

"I SURE WISH MRS. WILSON WOULD BRING YOU SOME MORE SOUP. I'M GETTIN' PRETTY SICK OF DAD'S COOKIN'!"

"I'LL *ASK* HIM, HONEY: GEORGE, DO THESE ITCH?"

"SHE'S SURE GOT A CRAZY 'FRIGERATOR! IT'S JUST GOT ONE *GREAT BIG* ICE CUBE IN IT!"

"BOY, IT MUST *REALLY* BE COLD IN *YOUR* YARD!"

"LET'S FORGET THE WHOLE THING. OKAY?
HERE: PUT YOUR TOOTH IN YOUR POCKET."

"WELL, I DON'T THINK IT'S NO BUSINESS TRIP. I THINK HE'S RUNNIN' AWAY FROM HOME!"

"I **TOLD** YOU WHY! I DIDN'T WANNA GO CLEAR HOME!"

"ALL I DID WAS SAY 'WHOA!' AND
THE TAIL CAME OUT!"

"SEE? I *TOLD* YA I SPILLED GLUE IN THAT SHOE!"

" WELL, GOD, I GOOFED AGAIN ... "